# MOTORCYCLE

## ADULT COLORING BOOK DESIGNS

Custom Motorcycle

PATTERNS FOR RELAXATION AND STRESS RELIEF

Born to ride
Ride to live

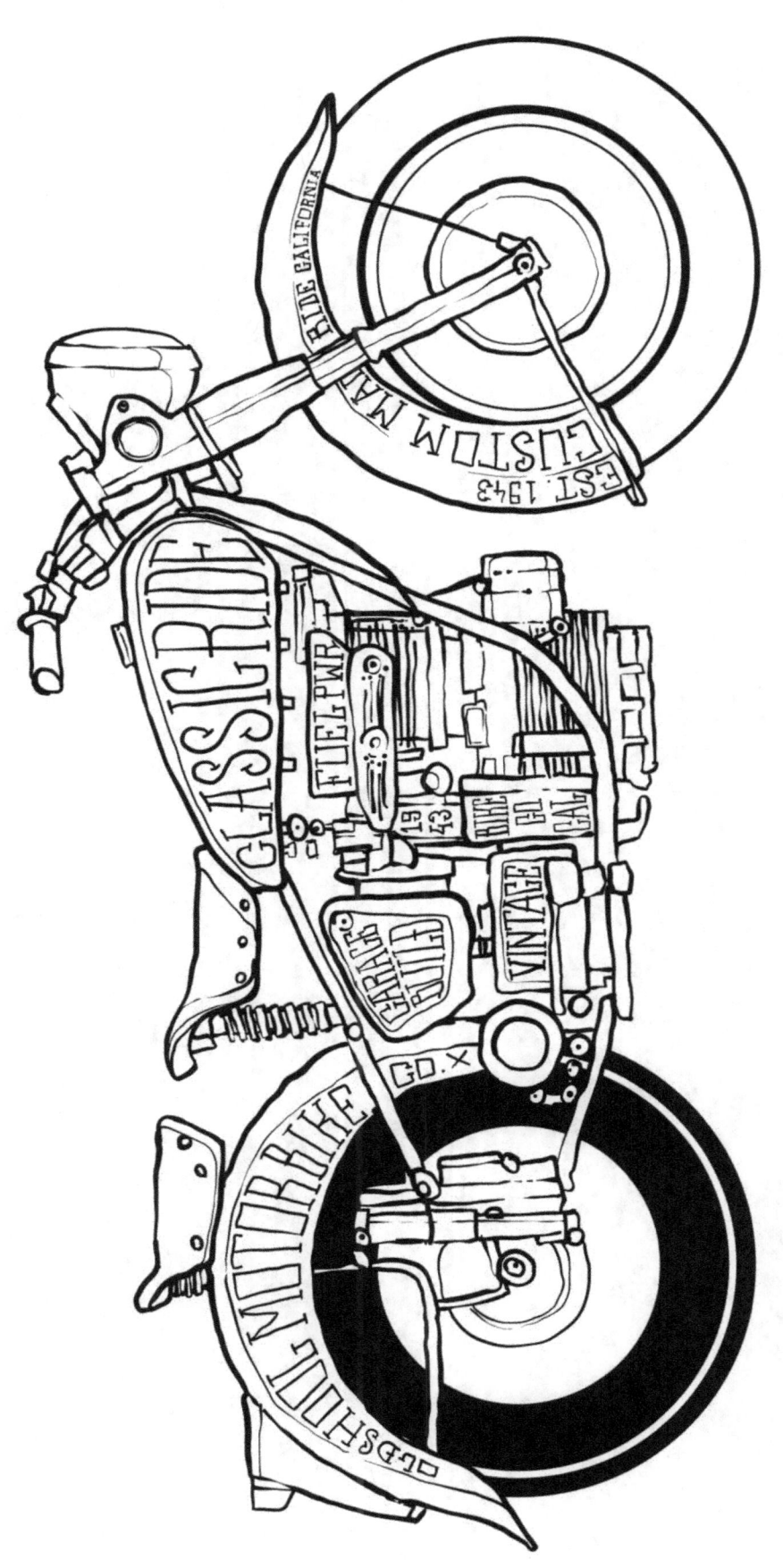

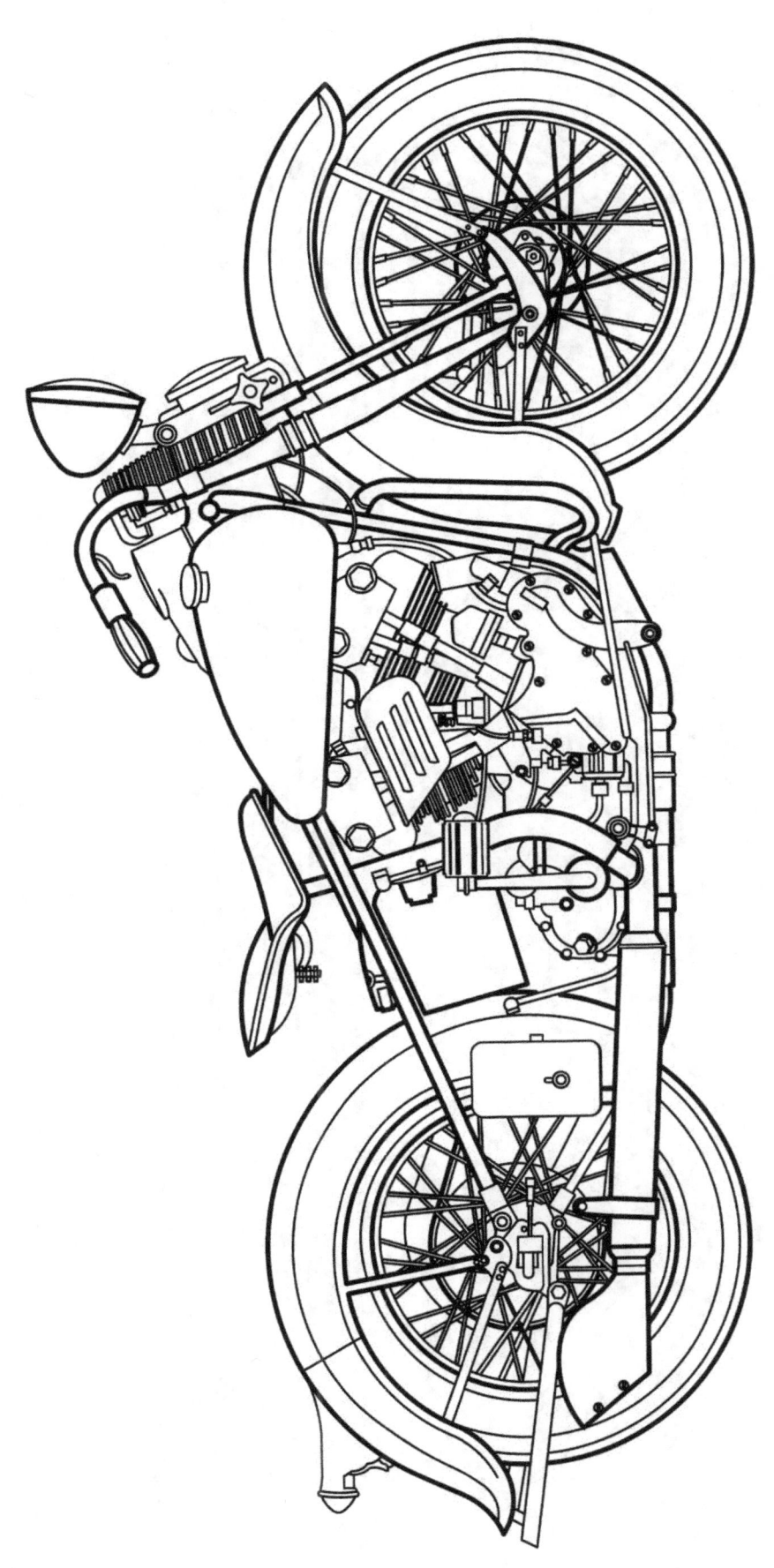

Original
CALIFORNIA RACE

MOTORCYCLE GARAGE

High Speed

MOTORCYCLE

Riding to win

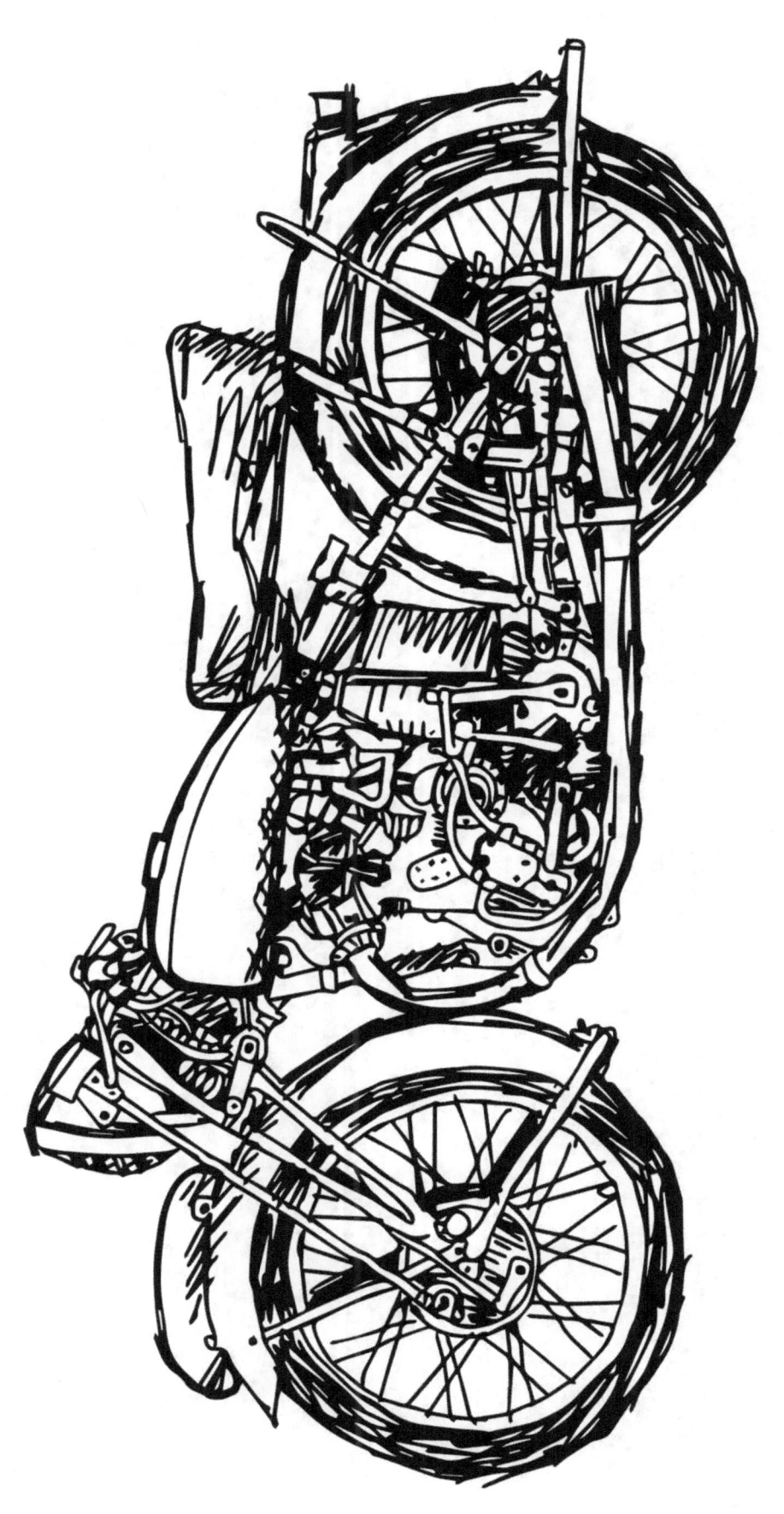

Never stop exploring

Born
to ride
Ride to
LIVE

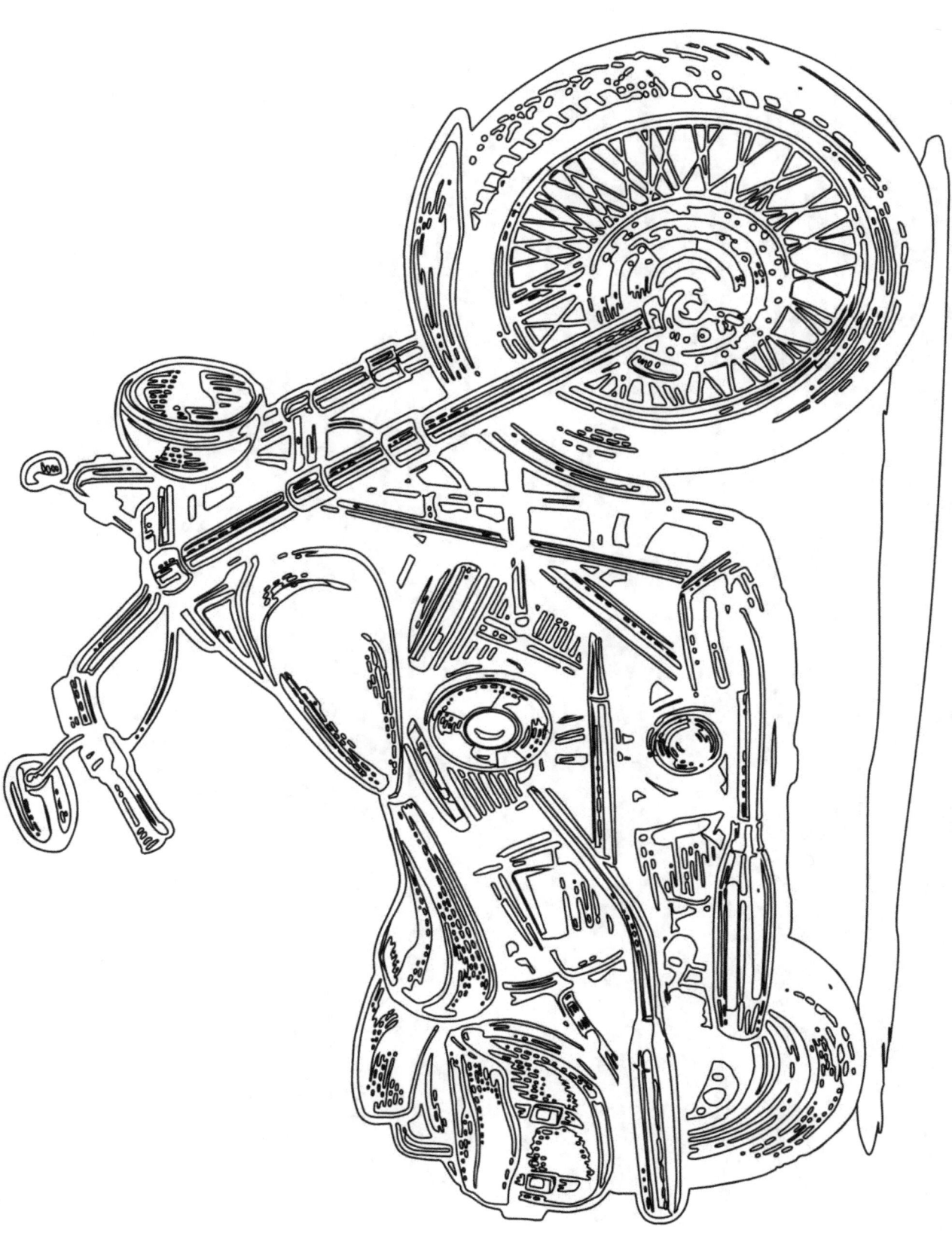

# American

# Motor

# Riders Club

## Live Fast Die Young

MOTORCYCLE

IRON HEART

Road    Speed

FIERY BLOOD

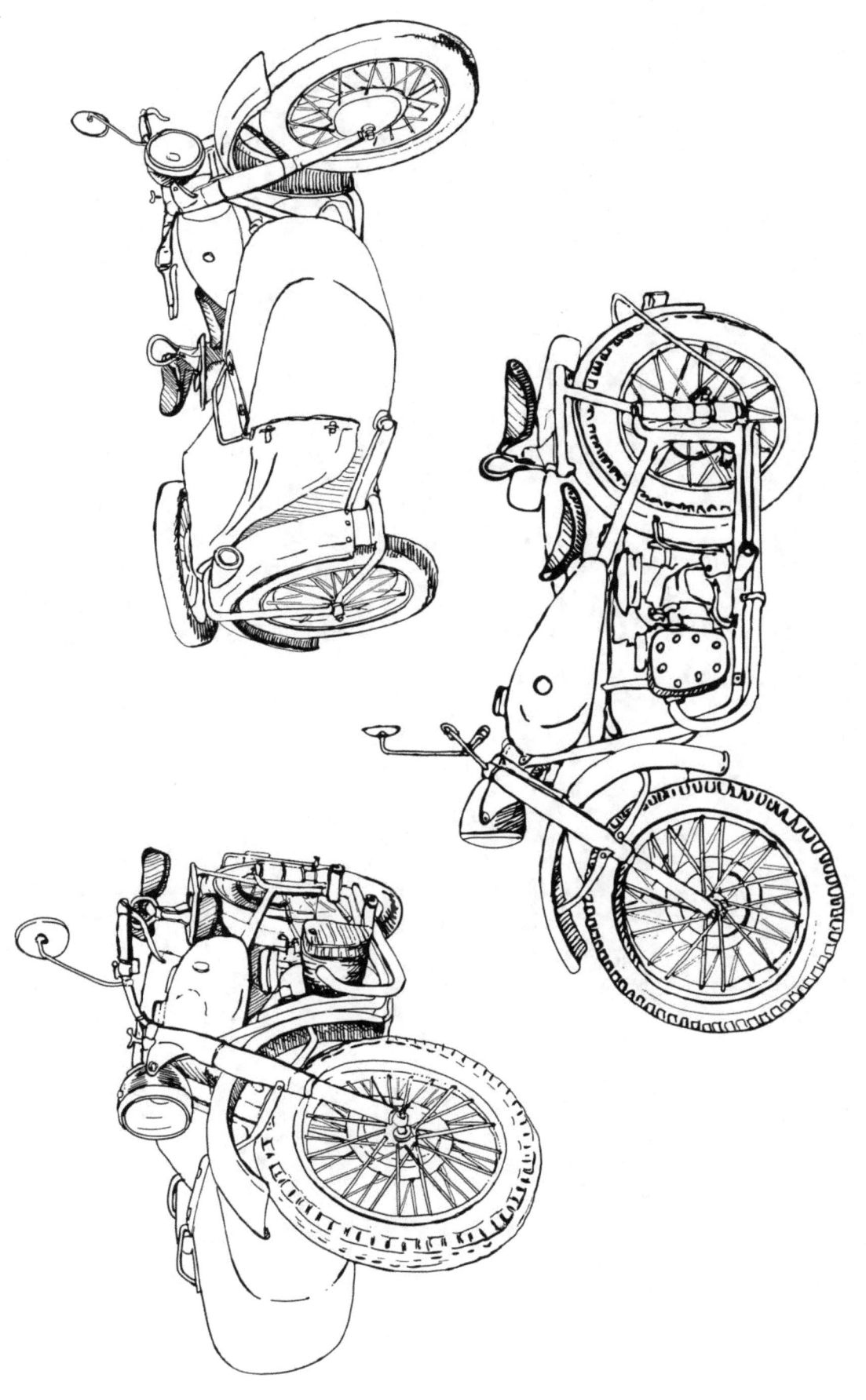

# California

**·1976·**

UNION SUPPLY CO.

# RIDE LIKE THE WIND
## LEGENDARY RIDERS
SUPER BUILT FOR SPEED POWER
IRON WHEELS
## SUPERIOR PERFORMANCE

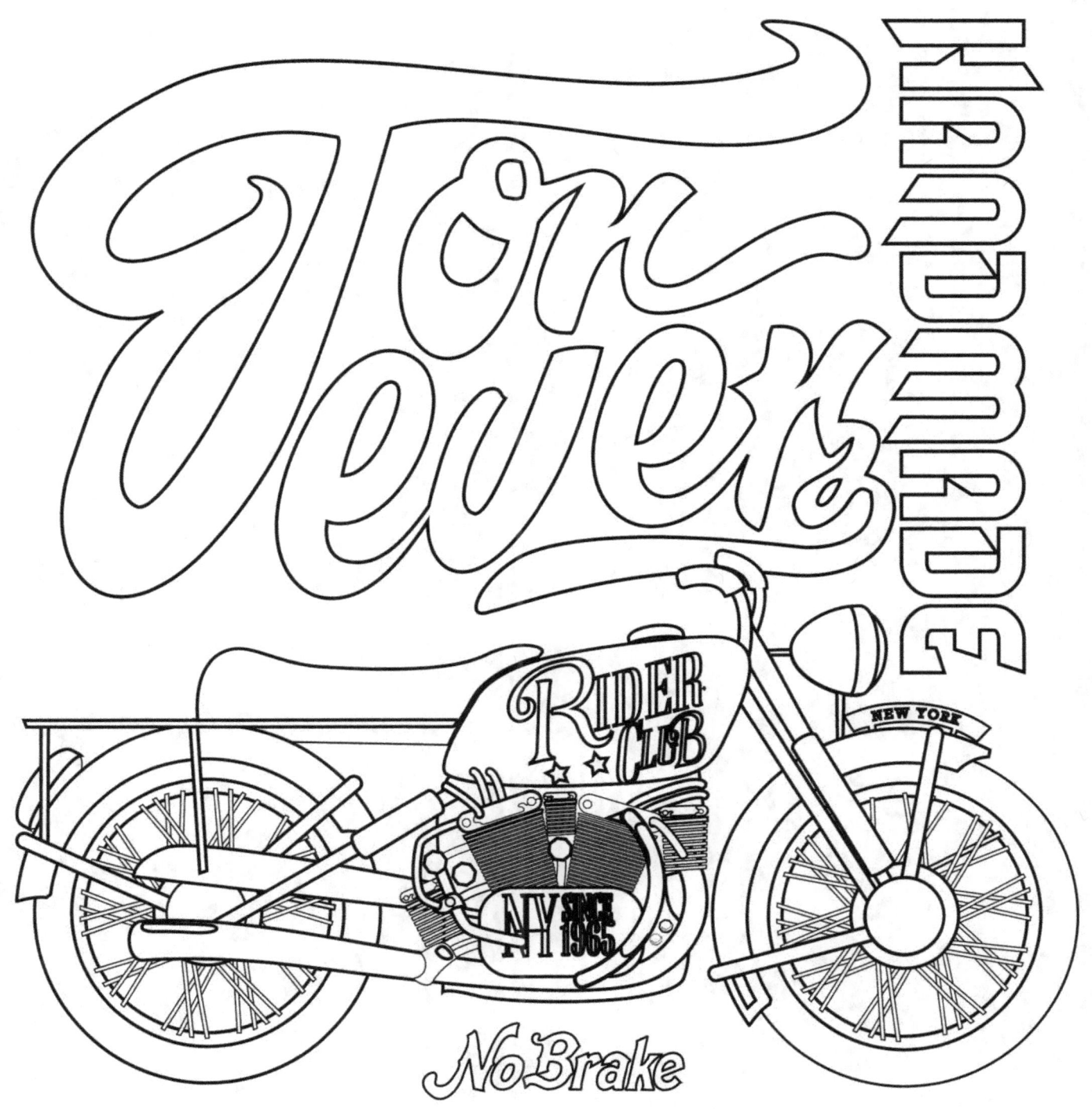

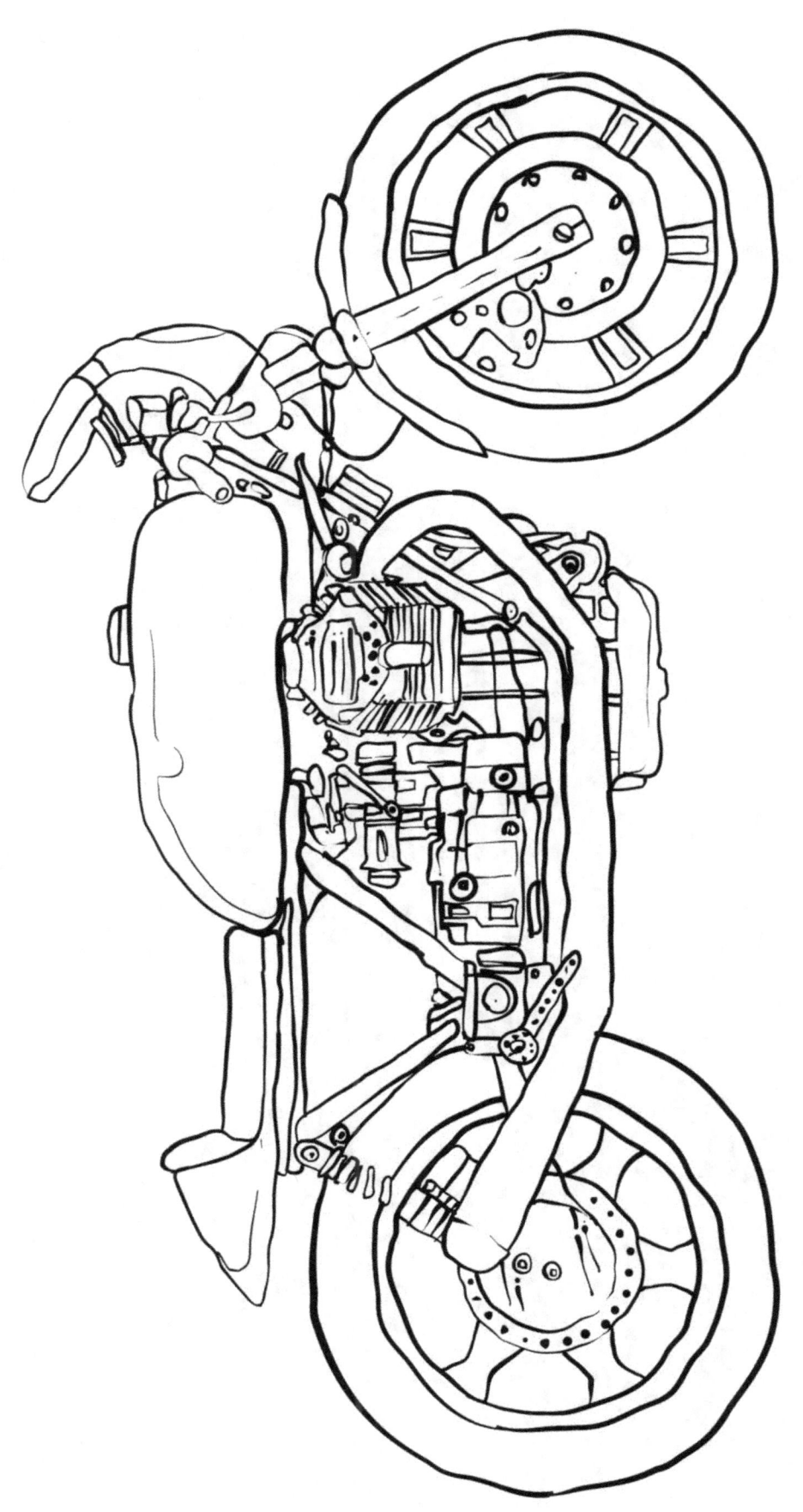